Book Title:

#1 Dropshipping Guide
to help you start your own Store
Successfully in 73 hours

Book Introduction:

Have you ever dreamed of starting your own online business, but didn't know where to begin? Look no further than dropshipping! This innovative business model allows you to sell products without holding any inventory, making it an ideal option for those who want to start a business with minimal upfront costs.

In this beginner's guide to dropshipping, we will take you through everything you need to know to start your own online store. From understanding what dropshipping is and how it works, to choosing your niche, setting up your website, sourcing products, and marketing your business, this guide covers it all.

One of the most attractive aspects of dropshipping is the flexibility it provides. You can operate your business from anywhere in the world, and all you need is an internet connection. This makes it a great option for those who want to travel or work from home.

Another advantage of dropshipping is that it allows you to test the waters before committing to a particular product or niche. You can easily add or remove products from your store without any additional costs, which means you can experiment with different products until you find the ones that work best for you.

In this guide, we will walk you through the steps you need to take to set up your dropshipping business. We'll start by discussing the basics of dropshipping and explaining how it works. We'll then move on to choosing a niche and selecting products to sell. We'll also cover how to create a

website for your business, and provide tips on how to optimize it for search engines.

We'll also go into detail on how to find and work with suppliers, including how to negotiate pricing and handle returns. Additionally, we'll provide guidance on how to market your business through social media, email marketing, and other channels.

Whether you're a total beginner or have some experience with e-commerce, this guide will give you the knowledge and tools you need to start your own successful dropshipping business. So, what are you waiting for? Let's get started!

Chapter 1. Understanding Dropshipping and How It Works

If you've heard of dropshipping but don't fully understand what it is or how it works, don't worry – you're not alone. In this chapter, we'll take a deep dive into the world of dropshipping and explore everything you need to know to get started.

What Is Dropshipping?

Dropshipping is a business model where the seller does not keep any inventory of the products they sell. Instead, the seller acts as an intermediary between the supplier and the customer, and the supplier ships the products directly to the customer on behalf of the seller. This means that the seller never physically handles the products they sell.

Dropshipping has become an increasingly popular way to start an online business, as it requires minimal upfront investment and allows sellers to test out different products without holding any inventory. In this chapter, we'll dive deeper into the workings of dropshipping and how it differs from traditional e-commerce models.

The Traditional E-Commerce Model

In traditional e-commerce models, the seller purchases products from a supplier or manufacturer, stores them in a warehouse, and then sells them to customers through an online store. The seller is responsible for storing, packaging, and shipping the products to the customer, and must handle any returns or exchanges. This requires a significant investment in inventory, storage, and shipping logistics, which can be a barrier to entry for new businesses.

The Dropshipping Model

In the dropshipping model, the seller does not hold any inventory. Instead, the seller creates an online store and markets products to customers. When a customer makes a purchase, the seller forwards the order details to a supplier, who then ships the product directly to the customer. The seller never physically handles the product, and the supplier is responsible for storing, packaging, and shipping the product.

Dropshipping allows sellers to operate an online store without the need for inventory or storage space, which significantly reduces the upfront costs associated with starting an online business. Sellers can focus on marketing and growing their business, without worrying about managing inventory or shipping logistics.

Benefits of Dropshipping

There are several benefits to the dropshipping model:

Low startup costs: As mentioned earlier, dropshipping requires minimal upfront investment. Sellers do not need to purchase inventory or store products, which means they can focus on building their website and marketing their products.

Flexible location: Because sellers do not need to store products, they can operate their business from anywhere in the world. All they need is an internet connection to manage their store.

Wide selection of products: Dropshipping allows sellers to offer a wide range of products without having to stock them in a physical location. This gives them the ability to test and sell products without the need for a large investment in inventory.

Scalability: With dropshipping, sellers can quickly scale their business as demand increases. Because they don't need to worry about inventory and storage costs, they can easily expand their product offerings and handle a high volume of orders without the need for additional resources.

Time savings: Dropshipping frees up a significant amount of time for sellers, allowing them to focus on building their brand, marketing their products, and providing exceptional customer service. This means they can spend less time on tedious tasks like inventory management and shipping logistics.

Customer convenience: Dropshipping allows customers to receive products directly from the supplier, which can lead to faster shipping times and lower shipping costs. This can result in higher customer satisfaction and loyalty. Overall, dropshipping can be a great option for entrepreneurs who want to start an online business with low overhead costs, minimal risk, and the ability to offer a wide range of products.

Low risk: With dropshipping, sellers only purchase products when they receive an order from

Chapter 2. Choosing Your Niche: Finding the Right Products to Sell

Once you understand the basics of dropshipping and how it works, the next step is to choose the right niche and the products you want to sell. Choosing the right niche is crucial because it will determine the products you sell and the audience you target. In this chapter, we'll discuss how to choose your niche and find the right products to sell.

Identify Your Interests and Passions

When choosing your niche, it's important to choose something you're passionate about. This will help you stay motivated and interested in your business, and it will also give you an advantage in understanding your audience's needs and preferences.

Start by brainstorming your interests and hobbies. Do you love fitness, beauty, technology, or pets? Make a list of the things that interest you and that you know well. This will help you narrow down your choices and find a niche that you're passionate about.

Evaluate Market Demand

Once you've identified your interests, the next step is to evaluate want to make sure that there is a demand for the products you want to sell, and that there is enough potential for growth and profitability.

You can start by researching popular products and trends within your niche. Check out online marketplaces like Amazon, eBay, and Etsy to see what products are popular and what people are buying. Look at customer reviews and ratings to get a sense of what people like and dislike about certain products.

You can also use keyword research tools like Google AdWords Keyword Planner or Ubersuggest to see what people are searching for related to your niche. This will help you understand what people are interested in and what keywords you should focus on when creating your product listings.

Analyze Your Competition

Another important factor to consider when choosing your niche is the competition. Look at other businesses that sell similar products within your niche and analyze their pricing, marketing strategies, and customer reviews.

You want to find a balance between a niche that has high demand but low competition. If a niche has too much competition, it will be

from other businesses. On the other hand, if a niche has little competition, it could be an indication that there isn't enough demand for the products you want to sell.

When analyzing your competition, pay attention to the following:

Pricing: Look at how your competitors are pricing their products. Are they priced higher or lower than what you plan to sell your products for? If they are priced lower, it could be a sign that the niche is saturated and it may be difficult to compete on price.

Marketing: Take note of how your competitors are marketing their products. What channels are they using? What messaging are they using to target their audience? This information will be valuable when developing your own marketing strategy.

Customer reviews: Look at customer reviews on your competitors' websites, as well as on third-party sites like Amazon or Trustpilot. This will give you an idea of what customers like and dislike about your competitors' products.

Consider Profit Margins

When choosing your niche, it's important to consider profit margins. You want to choose products that have a decent profit on each sale. This will ensure that your business is sustainable and profitable in the long run.

To calculate your profit margin, you need to subtract the cost of the product from the selling price and divide the result by the selling price. For example, if you sell a product for $50 and it costs you $30 to purchase and ship the product to your customer, your profit margin would be:

($50 - $30) / $50 = 40%

This means that you make a profit of $20 on each sale, which is 40% of the selling price.

When choosing products to sell, look for products with a profit margin of at least 30%. This will give you enough room to cover your business expenses and make a reasonable profit on each sale.

Consider Shipping Costs

Shipping costs are another factor to consider when choosing your niche and products to sell. Since you're not holding any inventory, you'll need to factor in the cost of shipping your products to your customers size and weight of your products, shipping costs can vary greatly. You may also need to factor in international shipping costs if you plan on selling to customers outside of your country.

To keep shipping costs low, consider selling products that are lightweight and easy to ship. You can also work with suppliers who offer free shipping or low-cost shipping options.

Look for Repeat Business Opportunities

Finally, when choosing your niche and products to sell, look for opportunities for repeat business. Selling products that customers need to replace regularly, or that have complementary products, can help you build a loyal customer base and increase your sales over time.

For example, if you sell pet supplies, you could sell products like pet food, toys, and grooming supplies that customers will need to replace regularly. You could also sell products like pet beds or crates that complement the products you already sell.

In conclusion, choosing the right niche and products to sell is crucial to the success of your dropshipping business. By identifying your interests and passions, evaluating market demand, analyzing your competition, considering profit margins and shipping costs, and looking for repeat business opportunities, you can choose a niche that is profitable and sustainable in the long run.

Chapter 3. Identifying Your Target Audience: Who You'll Be Selling To

When starting a dropshipping business, it's important to know who your target audience is. Your target audience is the group of people who are most likely to be interested in the products you're selling. Identifying your target audience is essential for creating a marketing strategy that will reach the right people and generate sales.

Here are some steps to help you identify your target audience:

Define Your Product

The first step in identifying your target audience is to define your product. What are you selling? What are the features and benefits of your product? What problem does it solve for your customers?

Defining your product will help you understand who your ideal customer is and what their needs and preferences are. For example, if you're selling pet products, your ideal customer might be a pet owner who is looking for high-quality and affordable products to keep their pets healthy and happy.

Conduct Market Research

Once you've defined your product, the next step is to conduct market research. Market research is the process of gathering information about your target audience, your competitors, and your industry.

To conduct market research, you can use a variety of tools and techniques,

Focus groups

-*Social media analytics*

-*Online forums and communities*

-*Industry reports and studies*

Market research can help you understand your target audience's demographics, psychographics, behavior, and preferences. This information can be used to create buyer personas, which are fictional representations of your ideal customers based on real data and insights.

Create Buyer Personas

Creating buyer personas can help you visualize and understand your target audience better. A buyer persona is a detailed profile of your ideal customer, including their age, gender, income, interests, values, goals, challenges, and purchasing behavior.

To create buyer personas, you can use the information you gathered from your market research, as well as your own intuition and experience. You can also use online tools and templates to create professional-looking buyer personas.

Having clear and detailed buyer personas can help you tailor your marketing messages, product offerings, and customer service to meet the needs and preferences of your target audience. This can help you build stronger relationships with your customers and increase your sales and revenue.

Analyze Your Competition

Another important step in identifying your target audience is to analyze your competition. Who else is selling similar products? What are their strengths and weaknesses? How are they positioning their brand and products?

Analyzing your competition can help you differentiate yourself and find a unique value proposition that will appeal to your target audience. It can also help you identify gaps and opportunities in the market that you can exploit to your advantage after you've identified your target audience, created buyer personas, and analyzed your competition, it's time to test and refine your marketing strategy. This is an ongoing process that involves measuring and analyzing your results, and making adjustments based on what works and what doesn't.

Here are some ways to test and refine your marketing strategy:

A/B testing: A/B testing is the process of comparing two versions of a marketing element, such as a landing page or email, to see which one performs better. This can help you optimize your messaging, design, and call-to-action to maximize conversions.

Analytics: Analytics tools, such as Google Analytics, can help you track and analyze your website traffic, user behavior, and conversion rates. This can help you identify areas of improvement and opportunities for growth.

Customer feedback: Gathering feedback from your customers, through surveys or reviews, can help you understand their needs and preferences better. This can help you improve your products and customer service, and create a more personalized shopping experience.

Social media: Social media platforms, such as Facebook and Instagram, can be powerful tools for reaching and engaging with your target audience. By monitoring your social media analytics and engagement, you can identify what content resonates with your audience and adjust your strategy accordingly.

Conclusion

In conclusion, identifying your target audience is a critical step in building a successful dropshipping business. By defining your product, conducting market research, creating buyer personas, analyzing your competition, and testing and refining your marketing strategy, you can attract and retain loyal customers and achieve long-term growth and profitability.

Chapter 4. Setting Up Your Online Store: Building a Website That Sells

Now that you've identified your niche and target audience, it's time to set up your online store. Your website is the face of your business and the primary channel for selling your products, so it's important to create a professional, user-friendly, and engaging website that can attract and convert visitors into customers.

In this chapter, we'll guide you through the process of building a website that sells, from choosing a platform and domain name, to designing and optimizing your website for conversions.

Choose a Platform

The first step in setting up your online store is to choose a platform that can host and manage your website. There are several e-commerce platforms available, each with their own features, pricing, and customization options.

Here are some popular e-commerce platforms you can

Shopify

Shopify is a popular e-commerce platform that offers an all-in-one solution for building and managing an online store. It provides a range of features, including customizable templates, payment processing, inventory management, and marketing tools. Shopify also offers a range of pricing plans, starting from $29 per month, depending on your business needs and budget.

WooCommerce

WooCommerce is a popular e-commerce plugin for WordPress that enables you to turn your website into an online store. It offers a range of features, including customizable templates, payment processing, inventory management, and shipping options. WooCommerce is free to use, but you will need to pay for web hosting and additional extensions.

BigCommerce

BigCommerce is another popular e-commerce platform that offers a range of features, including customizable, inventory management, and marketing tools. It also offers built-in SEO and social media integration, as well as multi-channel selling options. BigCommerce offers a range of pricing plans, starting from $29.95 per month, depending on your business needs and budget.

Choose a Domain Name

Once you've chosen your platform, you'll need to choose a domain name for your website. Your domain name is the web address that customers will use to access your website, so it's important to choose a name that is memorable, relevant to your business, and easy to spell and pronounce.

When choosing a domain name, consider the following tips:

Keep it short and simple: Choose a name that is easy to type and remember. Avoid using hyphens or numbers, as these can make your domain name confusing and hard to remember.

Make it relevant: Choose a name that reflects your business and niche. This can help customers remember your website and associate it

finalizing your domain name, make sure it is available and not already registered by another business. You can use domain name registrars such as GoDaddy or Namecheap to search for available domain names and register your chosen name.

Design Your Website

Once you've chosen your platform and domain name, it's time to design your website. Your website should be visually appealing, user-friendly, and optimized for conversions. Here are some tips for designing your website:

Choose a theme: Your e-commerce platform should offer a range of customizable themes or templates that you can use to design your website. Choose a theme that is relevant to your niche and reflects your brand.

Simplify navigation: Make sure your website is easy to navigate and that visitors can find what they're looking for quickly. Use clear and concise menus, and include search functionality to make it easier for customers to find products.

Optimize for mobile: With more people using their smartphones to shop online, it's important to optimize your website for mobile devices. Choose a mobile-friendly theme.

Include high-quality product images: When it comes to e-commerce, high-quality product images are essential. Use high-resolution images that showcase your products in the best possible light, and include multiple images from different angles.

Create clear and concise product descriptions: Your product descriptions should be clear, concise, and highlight the benefits of your products. Use bullet points to break up long paragraphs, and include any relevant information such as sizing or materials.

Include trust signals: Trust signals, such as customer reviews, security badges, and social proof, can help to build trust with potential customers and encourage them to make a purchase.

Set Up Payment Processing

Once you've designed your website, it's time to set up payment processing. Your e-commerce platform should offer a range of payment processing options, including credit cards, PayPal, and other popular payment methods.

To set up payment processing, you will need to create a merchant account with a payment gateway provider such as Stripe or PayPal. You will also need to ensure that compliant with PCI-DSS (Payment Card Industry Data Security Standard) regulations. This includes implementing SSL (Secure Sockets Layer) encryption to protect customer data, and ensuring that your website is regularly scanned for vulnerabilities.

Set Up Shipping and Fulfillment

One of the advantages of dropshipping is that you don't need to worry about storing, packing, and shipping your products. Instead, your supplier will handle these tasks for you. However, it's important to set up your shipping and fulfillment process to ensure that your customers receive their orders in a timely and efficient manner.

To set up shipping and fulfillment, you will need to choose a shipping carrier, such as USPS, FedEx, or UPS, and determine your shipping rates and policies. You should also create a process for communicating with your supplier and updating customers on the status of their orders.

Launch Your Website

Once you've set up your website, payment processing, and shipping and fulfillment, it's time to launch your website and start promoting your products. Here are some tips for launching your website:

Conduct a soft launch: Before launching your website to a soft launch to test your website and ensure that everything is working as it should be. Invite friends and family to test your website and provide feedback, and make any necessary adjustments before launching to the public.

Create a launch plan: Develop a launch plan to promote your website and generate buzz around your products. This may include social media promotions, email marketing, and advertising campaigns.

Offer incentives: To encourage people to visit your website and make a purchase, consider offering incentives such as discounts or free shipping for a limited time.

Monitor your analytics: Once your website is live, it's important to monitor your analytics to see how your website is performing. Use tools such as Google Analytics to track traffic, conversion rates, and other key metrics, and make adjustments as needed.

Conclusion

Setting up an online store can be a daunting task, but with the right tools and strategies, it can be a highly rewarding venture. By choosing the right e-commerce platform, identifying your target audience, designing a user-friendly website, and setting up payment processing and shipping and fulfillment, you can launch a successful dropshipping business and start generating revenue. With perseverance, hard work, and a dedication to customer service, the sky is the limit for your online store.

If you want a dropshipping website done for you

-Free Hosting for 1 Year

-Free Domain name for 1 year

-Fully intergrated with Aliexpress, Alibaba, Amazon, Ebay etc

-Fully intergrated with payment platforms like paypal, Visa, Mastercard, etc

Whatsapp your website budget cost to +254 710 100 974 and we will gladly d one for yu at your budget.

Thank you!

Chapter 5: Finding Reliable Suppliers

One of the key aspects of running a successful dropshipping business is sourcing reliable and high-quality products from trustworthy suppliers. When selecting a supplier, it's important to consider factors such as product quality, pricing, shipping times, and customer service. In this chapter, we will explore how to find and evaluate potential suppliers to ensure that you are working with the best possible partners for your business.

Types of Suppliers

There are two main types of suppliers that you can work with when dropshipping: domestic and international. Domestic suppliers are based in your home country, while international suppliers are based in other countries.

Domestic suppliers may offer faster shipping times and lower shipping costs, but they may also have higher product prices. International suppliers, on the other hand, may offer lower product prices, but shipping times and costs may be higher.

When choosing a supplier, it's important to consider these factors and determine which option makes the most sense for your business.

Finding Suppliers

There are several ways to find potential suppliers for your dropshipping business. Here are a few methods to consider:

Online directories: There are several online directories that list suppliers, such as AliExpress, SaleHoo, and Worldwide Brands. These directories allow you to search for suppliers by product category, location, and other criteria.

Trade shows: Attending trade shows is another way to find potential suppliers. Trade shows allow their products first-hand. Some popular trade shows for ecommerce businesses include the Canton Fair in China, the National

Hardware Show in the US, and the Autumn Fair in the UK.

Referrals: You can also ask for referrals from other businesses in your industry or from friends and family who may have connections to suppliers.

Evaluating Suppliers

Once you have identified potential suppliers, it's important to evaluate them to ensure that they are reliable and trustworthy partners for your business. Here are some factors to consider when evaluating suppliers:

Product quality: The quality of the products is a key factor in determining whether a supplier is a good fit for your business. Consider ordering a sample product to evaluate the quality before placing a larger order.

Pricing: Pricing is another important factor to consider when evaluating suppliers. Compare the prices of different suppliers to ensure that you are getting a fair price for the products you want to sell.

Shipping times: Shipping times can have a significant impact on customer satisfaction. Make sure that your suppliers can provide reliable and timely shipping.

Customer service: Good customer service is essential when working with a supplier. Make sure that the supplier is responsive to your inquiries and can address any issues that may arise.

Working with Suppliers

Once you have chosen a supplier, it's important to establish a good working relationship. Here are some tips for working with suppliers:

Communicate regularly: Maintain open and regular communication with your supplier to ensure that you are on the same page and that any issues are addressed promptly.

Place small orders initially: To minimize risk, consider placing a small order initially to evaluate the supplier's quality, pricing, and shipping times.

Negotiate pricing: Negotiate with your supplier to get the best possible price for the products you want to sell.

Consider working with multiple suppliers: steady supply of products, it's a good idea to work with multiple suppliers. This can also help you negotiate better prices and ensure that you have backup options in case one supplier has issues.

Build a strong relationship: Building a strong relationship with your supplier can lead to better prices, more reliable shipping, and better customer service. Consider sending them regular orders, paying on time, and providing feedback on their products and services.

Dropshipping Platforms

In addition to working with individual suppliers, there are also dropshipping platforms that can help you find and work with suppliers. These platforms act as intermediaries between you and the supplier, handling the logistics of shipping and order fulfillment. Some popular dropshipping platforms include:

AliExpress: This is a popular platform for finding and sourcing products from suppliers in China.

Oberlo: This platform is designed specifically for Shopify users and allows you to easily import products from AliExpress.

SaleHoo: This platform provides access to a directory of suppliers and also offers training and support for ecommerce businesses.

Doba: This platform connects you with suppliers and also provides product data and inventory management tools.

When choosing a dropshipping platform, consider the types of products and suppliers available, the pricing and fees, and the level of support and training provided.

Conclusion

Sourcing products is a critical step in setting up a successful dropshipping business. By following the steps outlined in this chapter, you can find reliable and high-quality suppliers that can help you build a profitable online store. Remember to evaluate suppliers carefully, communicate regularly, and consider using dropshipping platforms to streamline the process. With the right products and suppliers in place, you'll be well on your way to running a successful dropshipping business.

Chapter 6. Managing Your Inventory: Staying on Top of Stock Levels

One of the biggest challenges in dropshipping is managing inventory. Unlike traditional retail businesses where you have physical control over your stock, in dropshipping, you rely on your suppliers to fulfill orders. This can make it difficult to keep track of stock levels and ensure that you always have enough inventory to meet customer demand. In this chapter, we'll explore some strategies for managing your inventory and staying on top of stock levels.

Use inventory management software

One of the most effective ways to manage your inventory is to use inventory management software. This software can help you keep track of stock levels, monitor sales, and set up alerts when inventory levels are low. Some popular inventory management software options include:

TradeGecko: This software allows you to manage inventory across multiple sales channels and also provides analytics and reporting tools.

Skubana: This software integrates with multiple sales channels and can help you manage inventory, orders, and shipping.

Sellbrite: This software is designed specifically for ecommerce businesses and can help you manage inventory, orders, and listings.

When choosing inventory management software, consider your budget, the size of your business, and the features that are most important to you.

Set up automatic reorder points

Another strategy for managing inventory is to set up automatic reorder points. This involves setting a threshold for each product at which point you will automatically reorder from your supplier. For example, if you sell a product that has a high demand, you might set an automatic reorder point at 50% of your current stock level. This way, you can ensure that you always have enough inventory on hand to meet customer demand.

Monitor sales and adjust inventory levels

Another key strategy for managing inventory is to monitor sales and adjust inventory levels accordingly. By tracking sales data, you can identify which products are selling well and which products are not. This can help you make informed decisions about which products to restock and which products to remove from your store.

Communicate with your suppliers

Finally, it's important to communicate regularly with your suppliers to ensure that they can keep up with your demand. This can involve discussing lead times, minimum order quantities, and any other logistics involved in the fulfillment process. By building a strong relationship with your suppliers and keeping open lines of communication, you can ensure that your inventory levels stay in check.

Conclusion

Managing inventory is a critical component of running a successful dropshipping business. By using inventory management software, setting up automatic reorder points, monitoring sales, and communicating regularly with your suppliers, you can ensure that you always have enough inventory on hand to meet customer demand. Remember to track inventory levels regularly and make adjustments as needed to avoid stockouts and keep your customers happy.

Chapter 7: Marketing Your Store: Getting the Word Out About Your Business

Now that you've set up your online store and sourced your products, it's time to start promoting your business and getting customers to your website. Marketing is a crucial part of any business, and dropshipping is no exception. In this chapter, we'll explore different strategies and channels you can use to market your store effectively.

Social Media Marketing

Social media has become a powerful marketing tool for businesses of all sizes. With billions of people using social media platforms every day, it's a great way to reach potential customers and build brand awareness. Here are some tips for using social media to promote your dropshipping store:

> *Choose the right platform:* Different social media platforms have different demographics and user behaviors. For example, if you're targeting younger

audiences, platforms like Instagram and TikTok may be more effective. If you're targeting professionals, LinkedIn may be a better fit.

Post regularly: Consistency is key when it comes to social media. Make sure to post regularly and engage with your followers.

Use high-quality visuals: Social media is a visual platform, so it's important to use high-quality images and videos to showcase your products.

Collaborate with influencers: Influencer marketing is a popular way to reach new audiences. Consider partnering with influencers who align with your brand to promote your products.

Email Marketing

Email marketing is another effective way to reach your customers and keep them engaged with your brand. Here are some tips for using email marketing to promote your dropshipping store:

Build your email list: Encourage visitors to your website to sign up for your email list by offering a discount or freebie in exchange for their email address list: Segmenting your email list allows you to send targeted messages to specific groups of customers based on their interests or behavior. For example, you can send promotions for women's clothing to customers who have previously purchased women's clothing from your store.

Personalize your emails: Use the customer's name and previous purchase history to personalize your emails and make them feel more personalized.

Use a clear call-to-action (CTA): Make sure to include a clear CTA in your emails that encourages customers to take action, such as visiting your website or making a purchase.

Don't spam: Make sure to only send relevant and valuable content to your email list. Don't send too many emails and risk becoming spammy.

Search Engine Optimization (SEO)

SEO is the process of optimizing your website to rank higher in search engine results pages (SERPs). The higher your website ranks, the more likely people are to click through to your website. Here are some tips for optimizing your website for search engines:

> *Conduct keyword research:* Identify relevant keywords that your target audience is searching for and optimize your website's content around those keywords.

> *Optimize your website's structure:* Make sure your website is easy to navigate and has a clear structure that search engines can easily understand.

> *Create high-quality content:* High-quality content that provides value to your audience can help improve your website's rankings.

> *Build high-quality backlinks:* Backlinks are links from other websites to your website. Building high-quality backlinks can help improve your website's authority and rankings.

Paid Advertising

Paid advertising, such as Google Ads or Facebook Ads, can be an effective way to drive traffic to your website and reach new customers. Here are some tips for running successful paid advertising campaigns:

Set a budget: Determine how much you're willing to spend on advertising and set a budget that aligns with your business goals.

Define your target audience: Use targeting options to reach the right people with your ads.

Create compelling ad copy and visuals: Use eye-catching visuals and compelling ad copy to ent optimize your campaigns: Continuously monitor your ad performance and make adjustments as needed to improve your ROI.

Influencer Marketing

Influencer marketing involves partnering with influencers (people with a large following on social media) to promote your products or brand. Here are some tips for running successful influencer marketing campaigns:

Choose the right influencers: Make sure to partner with influencers who have a following that aligns with your target audience and brand values.

Set clear expectations: Clearly communicate your goals and expectations with the influencer before starting the campaign.

Give creative freedom: Allow the influencer to create content in their own style and voice to make the partnership feel authentic.

Track and measure results: Monitor the success of the campaign and measure ROI to determine if the partnership was effective.

Social Media Marketing

Social media marketing involves using social media platforms (such as Facebook, Instagram, and Twitter) to promote your products or brand. Here are some tips for running successful social media marketing campaigns:

Choose the right platforms: Identify the social media platforms where your target audience is most active and focus your efforts on those platforms.

Create engaging content: Use eye-catching visuals, videos, and engaging captions to grab people's attention and encourage them to engage with your content.

Use hashtags: Hashtags can help increase the visibility of your posts and make it easier for people to find your content.

Engage with your audience: Respond to comments and messages promptly to build a relationship with your audience and increase brand loyalty.

Conclusion

In conclusion, marketing your dropshipping store requires a multi-faceted approach that combines various strategies and tactics. By understanding your target audience, creating a strong brand identity, and utilizing effective marketing channels, you can drive traffic to your store and increase sales. Remember to continuously monitor and adjust your marketing efforts to ensure they are aligned with your business goals and deliver a strong ROI.

Chapter 8. Optimizing Your Product Listings: How to Write Product Descriptions that Convert

One of the keys to success in dropshipping is to create product listings that effectively communicate the value and benefits of your products to potential customers. In this chapter, we'll explore some strategies and techniques for writing product descriptions that convert.

Focus on Benefits, Not Features

When writing product descriptions, it's important to focus on the benefits of your products, not just their features. Benefits are the positive outcomes or solutions that your product provides to the customer, whereas features are the specific details and attributes of the product.

For example, if you're selling a fitness tracker, a feature might be "tracks heart rate", but the benefit is "monitors your heart rate to help you optimize your workouts and improve your health."

By focusing on the benefits of your products, you can help potential customers understand how your products can solve their problems or improve their lives.

Use Descriptive Language

Use descriptive language to paint a vivid picture of your products and their benefits. Use sensory words and descriptive phrases to help potential customers imagine using your product and experiencing its benefits.

For example, instead of saying "This is a high-quality leather bag", you could say "Experience the luxurious feel of genuine leather with this stylish and durable bag that will elevate your look and last for years to come."

Keep it Clear and Concise

While it's important to use descriptive language, it's also important to keep your product descriptions clear and concise. Use short sentences and paragraphs, bullet points, and headings to break up the text and make it easy to scan.

Make sure your descriptions are easy to read and understand, and avoid using technical jargon or overly complicated language.

Use Social Proof

Social proof refers to the phenomenon of people being influenced by the actions and opinions of others. You can use social proof to enhance the credibility and desirability of customer reviews and ratings in your product descriptions.

Potential customers are more likely to trust the opinions and experiences of others who have already purchased and used the product. Including reviews and ratings in your product descriptions can help to build trust and credibility with potential customers.

Include a Call-to-Action

A call-to-action (CTA) is a statement or prompt that encourages the reader to take a specific action, such as "buy now" or "add to cart". Including a clear and compelling CTA in your product descriptions can help to increase the chances of a potential customer making a purchase.

Make sure your CTA is prominent and easy to find, and use action-oriented language to create a sense of urgency and excitement.

Optimize for Search Engines

Optimizing your product listings for search engines can help increase visibility and drive more traffic to your online store. Include relevant keywords in your product titles and descriptions, and use meta descriptions and tags to make it easier for search engines to understand the content of your pages.

Be careful not to stuff your descriptions with too many keywords, as this can hurt the readability and overall quality of your product listings.

Show Product Variations

If your products come in different sizes, colors, or styles, make sure to show these variations in your product listings. This can help customers visualize the different options available to them and make it easier for them to find the product that best suits their needs.

Use High-Quality Images

High-quality images are essential for showcasing your products and giving potential customers a clear idea of what they can expect. Use multiple images from different angles, and make sure they are well-lit and show the product in context.

Consider hiring a professional photographer or using a high-quality camera to capture your product images. This can help make your products look more professional and appealing to potential customers.

Keep it Simple and Clear

Finally, it's important to keep your product descriptions simple and clear. Avoid using technical jargon or overly complex language that could confuse or turn off potential customers.

Instead, use simple and straightforward language that clearly conveys the benefits and features of your products. Make sure your descriptions are easy to scan and visually appealing, with clear headings, bullet points, and images.

Conclusion

Writing product descriptions that convert is an essential part of dropshipping success. By following the tips outlined in this chapter, you can create compelling and effective product descriptions that attract potential customers and drive sales.

Remember to focus on the benefits and features of your products, use descriptive language and visuals, include customer reviews and ratings, optimize for SEO, and keep your descriptions simple and clear.

With these strategies in place, you'll be well on your way to creating a successful dropshipping business that generates sales and profits for years to come.

Chapter 9: Fulfilling Orders: Shipping Products to Your Customers

Now that you've set up your dropshipping store and started receiving orders, it's time to fulfill those orders and ship products to your customers. This is a crucial step in the dropshipping process, as it directly affects customer satisfaction and can impact your business reputation.

In this chapter, we'll explore the key steps involved in fulfilling orders and shipping products to your customers, including selecting a shipping method, managing shipping costs, and handling returns and refunds.

Selecting a Shipping Method

The first step in shipping your products to customers is selecting a shipping method. This involves choosing a carrier or shipping service that will transport your products from your supplier's warehouse to your customer's doorstep.

There are many different shipping carriers and services available, including the United States Postal Service (USPS), FedEx, UPS, DHL, and more. Each carrier has its own rates, delivery times, and service options, so it's important to research and compare your options to find the best fit for your business.

When selecting a shipping method, consider factors such as the size and weight of your products, the shipping destination, and your customers' preferences. You may also want to offer multiple shipping options to give customers the flexibility to choose the delivery speed and cost that works best for them.

Managing Shipping Costs

Shipping costs are a significant expense for dropshipping businesses, so it's important to manage them carefully to ensure profitability. Here are some tips for managing shipping costs:

Negotiate rates with carriers: Many shipping carriers offer discounted rates for businesses that ship in high volumes or on a regular basis. Contact your carrier to inquire about discounts or negotiate a better rate.

Use shipping software: Shipping software can help you compare rates across different carriers, automate shipping labels and tracking, and streamline the shipping process.

Offer free shipping selectively: Offering free shipping can be a powerful marketing tool, but it can also eat into your profits. Consider offering free shipping for orders over a certain amount, or for certain products or customers.

Choose a Shipping Carrier

Once you have packaged the order, the next step is to choose a shipping carrier to transport the product to your customer. There are several shipping carriers available, each with its own advantages and disadvantages.

USPS: The United States Postal Service (USPS) is a popular option for many small businesses due to its affordability and reliability. USPS offers several shipping options, including First Class Mail, Priority Mail, and Priority Mail

Express. Each option has different delivery times and pricing, so be sure to choose the one that best fits your needs.

FedEx: FedEx is a private shipping company that offers a variety of shipping options, including express and ground shipping. FedEx is known for its fast delivery times and excellent customer service.

UPS: UPS is another popular private shipping company that offers a range of shipping options, including ground, air, and international shipping. UPS also provides package tracking and insurance options for added security.

DHL: DHL is an international shipping company that specializes in express shipping and logistics. DHL is a good option for businesses that need to ship products internationally, as it has a strong global network.

Notify the Customer

Once you have shipped the product, it is important to notify the customer that their order has been shipped. This can be done through email, text message, or the online platform you are using to sell your products. Be sure to include a tracking number so the customer can keep track of their shipment.

Follow Up with the Customer

After the customer has received their order, it is important to follow up with them to ensure they are satisfied with their purchase. This can be done through email or a phone call. If the customer has any issues or concerns, be sure to address them promptly to maintain a positive relationship with the customer.

Conclusion

Fulfilling orders is an important aspect of running a successful dropshipping business. By choosing reliable suppliers, packaging products securely, and selecting a shipping carrier that meets your needs, you can ensure that your customers receive their orders in a timely and efficient manner. With good communication and follow-up, you can also

build a loyal customer base that will continue
to support your business in the long run.

Chapter 10: Handling Returns and Customer Service: Keeping Your Customers Happy

In any business, it's essential to prioritize customer satisfaction. This is especially true in the dropshipping business model, where you rely on customer loyalty and positive reviews to grow your business. In this chapter, we will discuss the importance of customer service and how to handle returns to keep your customers happy.

Why Customer Service is Important in Dropshipping?

In dropshipping, you are essentially the middleman between the supplier and the customer. You don't have control over the quality of the products or the shipping process, so it's crucial to provide excellent customer service to compensate for these factors. Good customer service can help you differentiate your business from competitors and can lead to customer loyalty and positive reviews.

One of the best ways to provide good customer service is by being responsive and communicative. Responding promptly to customer inquiries and concerns can help build trust and improve the customer experience. You can also use customer feedback to improve your business operations and address any recurring issues.

Handling Returns in Dropshipping

As we discussed in the previous chapter, handling returns is an essential part of any business, including dropshipping. Although it can be challenging to manage returns when you don't have control over the shipping and fulfillment process, there are steps you can take to make it easier.

Firstly, it's essential to have a clear and transparent return policy. Make sure to include information on how long customers have to return a product, what condition the product must be in, and any fees associated with the return. You can also consider offering a satisfaction guarantee to give customers peace of mind when they make a purchase.

When a customer requests a return, respond promptly and professionally. Ask for a reason for the return and offer options for how to proceed, such as a replacement or refund. If the product is damaged or defective, offer to cover the cost of return shipping.

No matter how carefully you package and ship your products, there may be times when customers need to return or exchange their purchase. It's important to have a clear policy in place for handling returns and refunds to ensure a smooth and positive customer experience.

When a customer requests a return, respond promptly and professionally. Ask for a reason for the return and offer options for how to proceed, such as a replacement or refund. If the product is damaged or defective, offer to cover the cost of return shipping.

Once you receive the returned product, inspect it carefully to ensure that it meets your return policy requirements. If it does, process the refund or exchange promptly. If the customer is dissatisfied with the outcome, be prepared to negotiate a solution that works for both parties.

Remember, handling returns and refunds professionally can turn a negative experience into a positive one and can lead to repeat business and positive reviews.

Chapter 11: Growing Your Dropshipping Store

After you've successfully launched your dropshipping store and have a steady stream of sales, you may want to consider scaling your business to increase your revenue and profits. Here are some tips for growing your dropshipping store:

Expand Your Product Range: Once you've established a successful niche, consider expanding your product range to cater to a wider audience. Look for products that complement your existing products and have a proven track record of success in your market.

Increase Your Marketing Efforts: Invest in targeted advertising and social media campaigns to reach a wider audience. Consider partnering with influencers or running promotions to drive traffic to your store.

Optimize Your Website: As your store grows, it's important to continually optimize your website to improve the user experience and increase conversions. Test different layouts, product descriptions, and call-to-action buttons to see what works best for your audience.

Streamline Your Operations: As your business grows, you'll need to streamline your operations to ensure that you can handle the increased demand. Consider outsourcing tasks like customer service or order fulfillment to free up your time to focus on growing your business.

Diversify Your Sales Channels: In addition to your website, consider selling your products on other marketplaces like Amazon or eBay to reach a wider audience. This can also provide a safety net in case your website experiences any technical difficulties.

Build Relationships with Suppliers: As you grow, it's important to maintain good relationships with your suppliers to ensure that you can continue to source high-quality products at competitive prices. Consider negotiating bulk discounts or exclusive deals to give your business a competitive advantage.

Focus on Customer Retention: As your business grows, don't forget to focus on retaining your existing customers. Offer loyalty programs, discounts, and personalized recommendations to keep customers coming back.

Conclusion

Growing a dropshipping business takes time, effort, and a willingness to learn and adapt. By following the tips outlined in this chapter, you can start scaling your business and taking it to the next level. Remember to focus on your niche, stay organized, optimize your website and product listings, and provide excellent customer service

Chapter 12: Expanding Your Product Range:

Adding More Products to Your Store

Once you have your dropshipping business up and running, one of the best ways to grow your business is by expanding your product range. By adding more products to your store, you can attract a wider range of customers and increase your sales. But how do you go about adding new products to your store? In this chapter, we'll explore some strategies for expanding your product range and growing your business.

Identify Your Customers' Needs

The first step in expanding your product range is to identify your customers' needs. Who are your target customers, and what products are they looking for? Conduct market research to find out what products are in demand in your niche. You can use keyword research tools like Google AdWords to see what products people are searching for online. You can also check out your competitors to see what products they are selling and which ones are popular.

Source New Products

Once you have identified the products you want to sell, you need to find reliable suppliers. Look for suppliers that offer good quality products at competitive prices. You can use online directories like AliExpress, Oberlo, and SaleHoo to find suppliers in your niche. You can also attend trade shows and meet with manufacturers to find new products to sell.

Test Your Products

Before adding new products to your store, it's important to test them first. You can order samples from your suppliers to ensure that the products meet your quality standards. You can also test new products by adding them to your store on a trial basis. Use analytics tools to track sales and customer feedback to see if the products are popular.

Optimize Your Product Listings

When you add new products to your store, it's important to optimize your product listings. This includes writing compelling product descriptions, adding high-quality product images, and using relevant keywords. You can also create product videos to showcase your new products and increase engagement.

Cross-Sell and Up-Sell

Cross-selling and up-selling are two effective strategies for expanding your product range and increasing your sales. Cross-selling involves offering related products to customers who have already made a purchase.

Conduct Market Research

Before you start adding new products to your store, it's essential to conduct market research. You want to ensure that there's a demand for the products you're planning to sell. You can start by analyzing your existing customers' purchasing behavior, looking at industry trends, and studying your competitors' product offerings.

Another great way to gauge customer demand is by using keyword research tools such as Google Keyword Planner or Ahrefs. These tools can help you identify which products are popular and have high search volume.

Evaluate Your Suppliers

Once you have an idea of the products you want to sell, you need to evaluate your suppliers. It's crucial to choose reliable suppliers that offer high-quality products at a reasonable price.

You can start by contacting your existing suppliers to see if they offer the products you're interested in. If they don't, you can research other suppliers online. Consider factors such as their reputation, delivery times, and pricing. You can also reach out to other dropshippers in your niche to get recommendations on suppliers.

Add Products to Your Store

Once you've found suitable suppliers, you can start adding products to your online store. Make sure to include high-quality product images, detailed descriptions, and pricing information. You can also consider adding product reviews and ratings to help customers make informed decisions.

It's essential to organize your products into categories to make it easy for customers to navigate your store. Consider creating a featured products section or promoting your new products on your homepage.

Test Your Products

It's always a good idea to test your new products before adding them to your store permanently. You can do this by creating a small product listing and running a few ads to see how they perform. If the product sells well, you can consider adding it permanently to your store.

Monitor Your Sales and Customer Feedback

After you've added new products to your store, it's important to monitor your sales and customer feedback. You want to ensure that your new products are selling well and that customers are satisfied with their purchase.

Pay attention to customer reviews and ratings to see if there are any issues that need to be addressed. You can also use analytics tools to track your sales and see which products are the most popular.

Conclusion

Expanding your product range is an excellent way to grow your dropshipping business. However, it's essential to conduct thorough market research, evaluate your suppliers, and test your products before adding them permanently to your store. By following these steps, you can ensure that your new products are successful and contribute to your overall business growth.

Chapter 13: Managing Your Finances: Keeping Track of Your Income and Expenses

One of the most important aspects of running a successful dropshipping business is managing your finances. As a business owner, it's crucial to keep track of your income and expenses to ensure that you're profitable and to make informed decisions about the future of your business.

In this chapter, we'll cover the basics of managing your finances, including:

1. Tracking your income
2. Keeping track of your expenses
3. Calculating your profit margin
4. Understanding taxes
5. Hiring an accountant

Tracking Your Income

The first step in managing your finances is to track your income. This includes all the money that comes into your business, such as sales revenue, shipping fees, and any other income streams.

To track your income, you can use a simple spreadsheet or accounting software. You should record every sale and include the amount of the sale, the date, and any associated fees.

It's also important to keep track of any refunds or chargebacks that you receive. This will help you to understand the overall health of your business and make adjustments as necessary.

Managing Your Expenses

Along with tracking your income, it is important to keep track of your expenses as a dropshipper. This includes all costs related to running your business, such as website hosting fees, advertising costs, and product costs.

One of the biggest advantages of dropshipping is that it allows you to avoid many of the traditional costs associated with running a business, such as renting a warehouse or purchasing inventory upfront. However, there are still a number of expenses that you will need to account for as a dropshipper.

To manage your expenses effectively, it is a good idea to create a budget for your business. This should include all of your expected expenses, as well as any contingencies for unexpected costs. You can use accounting software to help you create and track your budget, and to ensure that you are staying within your means.

Another important consideration when managing your expenses is to stay on top of your supplier costs. It is essential to negotiate favorable terms with your suppliers and to regularly review your pricing to ensure that you are getting the best possible deal.

Tax Considerations

As a business owner, it is also important to be aware of your tax obligations. Depending on your location and the size of your business, you may be required to collect and remit sales tax on your sales.

It is a good idea to consult with a tax professional to ensure that you are meeting all of your tax obligations as a dropshipper. They can help you to understand the relevant tax laws and regulations

Calculating Your Profit Margins

Your profit margin is the difference between the price you sell your products for and the cost of those products, including any shipping and handling fees. To calculate your profit margin, you need to know your gross profit and your net profit.

Gross profit is the difference between your revenue and the cost of your goods sold (COGS). To calculate your gross profit, subtract the COGS from your revenue. For example, if you sold $1,000 worth of products and your COGS were $600, your gross profit would be $400.

Net profit, on the other hand, takes into account all of your expenses, including operating expenses like rent, utilities, and marketing costs. To calculate your net profit, subtract all of your expenses from your gross profit. For example, if your gross profit is $400 and your expenses are $200, your net profit would be $200.

It's important to regularly calculate your profit margins, so you can ensure that you are pricing your products appropriately and making a profit. Ideally, you want to have a healthy profit margin that allows you to cover your expenses and invest in the growth of your business.

Budgeting for Expenses

Dropshipping may be a low-cost business model, but it's not free. There are still expenses you need to budget for, including website hosting, marketing costs, and the cost of your products. It's important to budget for these expenses in advance, so you can make informed decisions about the growth of your business.

To create a budget, start by listing all of your fixed expenses, such as your website hosting fees, and your variable expenses, such as marketing costs. You should also include an allowance for unexpected expenses, such as returns or damaged products. Once you have a list of all your expenses, estimate how much each one will cost you on a monthly basis. Then, add up all of your expenses to get your total monthly budget.

Managing Your Cash Flow

Cash flow is the lifeblood of any business, and it's especially important for dropshippers. Since you don't hold any inventory, you only pay for your products once you have made a sale. However, this also means that you need to be careful with your cash flow, so you can pay your suppliers on time and avoid any disruptions to your business.

One way to manage your cash flow is to create a cash flow forecast. This involves projecting your future income and expenses, so you can anticipate any cash flow issues and take action to address them before they become a problem. To create a cash flow forecast, start by listing your expected income for each month. Then, list all of your expenses, including your cost of goods sold, marketing expenses, and any other fixed and variable expenses. Once you have a list of your income and expenses, subtract your expenses from your income to get your projected cash flow for each month.

Conclusion

Managing your finances is a critical aspect of running a successful dropshipping business. By understanding your profit margins, budgeting for expenses, and managing your cash flow, you can make informed decisions about the future of your business and ensure its long-term success. Remember to regularly review your finances, so you can make adjustments as needed and keep your business on track.

Chapter 14: Dealing with Legal and Tax Issues:

Navigating the Legal Landscape of Dropshipping

Starting a dropshipping business may seem like a simple and straightforward process, but there are various legal and tax considerations that you need to be aware of. Failing to comply with the laws and regulations can result in legal issues, penalties, and even the closure of your business. Therefore, it is essential to understand the legal and tax landscape of dropshipping before launching your store.

Legal Considerations for Dropshipping Business

The legal considerations for dropshipping business vary by location and can be complex. However, here are some key legal issues that you need to consider when starting a dropshipping business:

Business Registration: You need to register your business with the relevant authorities in your jurisdiction. This can include registering your business name, obtaining a tax ID number, and applying for any necessary licenses or permits.

Product Liability: As a dropshipper, you are responsible for the products that you sell. Therefore, it is crucial to ensure that your suppliers are reputable and provide high-quality products. You may also need to purchase product liability insurance to protect your business from any claims resulting from defective products.

Intellectual Property: It is essential to avoid infringing on the intellectual property rights of others. This includes trademarks, copyrights, and patents. Make sure to research the trademarks and copyrights of the products you plan to sell to avoid any legal disputes.

Privacy and Data Protection: Your website should comply with privacy and data protection laws, such as the General Data Protection Regulation (GDPR). This includes obtaining consent from your customers before collecting their personal information and ensuring that their data is secure.

Tax Considerations for Dropshipping Business

Dropshipping can also have significant tax implications, and it is essential to understand the tax laws in your jurisdiction. Here are some key tax considerations for dropshipping business:

> ***Sales Tax:*** As a dropshipper, you may be responsible for collecting and remitting sales tax on behalf of your customers. The sales tax laws vary by location, and it is crucial to understand the requirements in your jurisdiction

> *Income Tax:* Your dropshipping business income is taxable, and you will need to report it on your tax return

Business Structure

One of the first legal considerations you'll need to make when starting your dropshipping business is your business structure. There are several options available, including sole proprietorship, partnership, LLC, and corporation.

A sole proprietorship is the simplest and most common business structure. It's easy to set up and requires minimal paperwork. As the sole owner, you'll be responsible for all business activities, profits, and losses. However, you'll also be personally liable for any debts or legal issues that arise.

A partnership is a business structure where two or more individuals share ownership and responsibility for the business. In a partnership, profits and losses are shared between partners, and each partner is personally liable for any legal or financial issues that arise.

An LLC, or limited liability company, is a popular business structure for dropshipping businesses. It provides personal liability protection for the owners while allowing them to benefit from the business's tax advantages. LLCs also offer flexibility in management and structure.

A corporation is a separate legal entity that can be owned by shareholders. Corporations offer liability protection and tax benefits, but they require more paperwork and formalities than other business structures.

Chapter 15: Avoiding Common Pitfalls: Learning from the Mistakes of Others

As with any business, dropshipping comes with its own set of challenges and potential pitfalls. By learning from the mistakes of others, you can avoid common errors and set yourself up for success.

Here are some of the most common mistakes that dropshippers make, and how you can avoid them:

Choosing the Wrong Niche: One of the biggest mistakes that new dropshippers make is choosing a niche that is too broad or too competitive. Instead, focus on a specific niche that has high demand and low competition. Do your research and use tools like Google Trends and Keyword Planner to find profitable niches.

Not Conducting Proper Due Diligence: Before choosing a supplier, make sure to do your due diligence. Check their reputation, read reviews, and ask for references. Avoid suppliers that have a history of late shipments, poor quality products, or bad customer service.

Failing to Test Products: It's important to test products before adding them to your store. Don't assume that just because a product is popular, it will sell well in your store. Test different products and monitor their performance to see which ones are the most profitable.

Ignoring Customer Service: Customer service is key to any successful business, and dropshipping is no exception. Make sure to respond to customer inquiries and complaints in a timely and professional manner. Consider using tools like chatbots or customer service software to streamline the process.

Underestimating Shipping Times: Shipping times can make or break your business. Be transparent with customers about shipping times and set realistic expectations. Consider using a shipping calculator on your website to help customers estimate delivery times.

Overlooking Marketing: Even if you have a great product, you need to market it effectively to attract customers. Don't overlook the importance of marketing in your business strategy. Consider using social media advertising, influencer marketing, or email marketing to promote your store.

Neglecting Your Finances: It's important to keep track of your finances and stay on top of your expenses and revenue. Neglecting your finances can lead to serious problems down the road. Use accounting software or hire an accountant to keep your books in order.

By avoiding these common mistakes and learning from the experiences of others, you can set yourself up for success in the world of dropshipping. Remember, dropshipping is a constantly evolving industry, and staying as a dropshipper, you're competing against other online retailers. It's important to offer competitive prices to attract and retain customers. However, you should also be mindful of your profit margins and ensure that you're not selling products at a loss.

Inadequate Customer Service: Customer service is essential in any business, including dropshipping. Providing excellent customer service can help you build a loyal customer base and generate positive reviews and word-of-mouth referrals. Respond promptly to customer inquiries, offer refunds or exchanges when necessary, and handle complaints professionally.

Failing to Manage Your Finances Properly: Managing your finances is crucial in any business, and dropshipping is no exception. Keep track of your income and expenses, pay taxes on time, and stay on top of your cash flow. Utilize accounting software or hire a bookkeeper if necessary.

Not Investing in Marketing: Marketing is key to promoting your dropshipping business and generating sales. Many dropshippers make the mistake of not investing enough in marketing. Utilize social media, email marketing, paid advertising, and other marketing strategies to reach your target audience and drive traffic to your website.

Choosing the wrong products to sell: One of the most common mistakes that dropshippers make is choosing the wrong products to sell. When choosing products, it's essential to consider factors such as demand, competition, and profit margins. You should also consider the size and weight of the products, as this can impact your shipping costs.

To avoid this pitfall, take the time to research your products thoroughly before adding them to your store. Look for products that are in high demand but have low competition, and make sure that the profit margins are sufficient to cover your expenses.

Ignoring the importance of branding: Branding is essential in any business, and dropshipping is no exception. Your brand is what sets you apart from your competitors and makes your store memorable to customers. Failing to invest in your branding can make it challenging to stand out in a crowded marketplace.

To avoid this pitfall, take the time to invest in your branding. This includes creating a logo, developing a unique brand voice, and using consistent branding across all of your marketing materials.

Not optimizing your website for conversions: Your website is your most important sales tool, and failing to optimize it for conversions can be a costly mistake. If your website is slow, difficult to navigate, or doesn't provide enough information about your products, you could be losing potential customers.

To avoid this pitfall, make sure that your website is optimized for conversions. This includes using clear calls to action, providing detailed product descriptions, and making sure that your website is easy to navigate.

Ignoring the importance of SEO: SEO (search engine optimization) is essential in any online business, and dropshipping is no exception. Without proper SEO, your website may not rank well in search engine results, which can make it challenging to attract new customers.

To avoid this pitfall, make sure that you invest in SEO. This includes optimizing your website for keywords related to your products, building high-quality backlinks, and ensuring that your website is mobile-friendly.

Ignoring Legal and Tax Obligations: Finally, it's essential to comply with all legal and tax obligations as a dropshipper. This includes registering your business, obtaining any necessary licenses

Conclusion

Dropshipping is a popular and profitable business model that has allowed many entrepreneurs to start their own successful online stores. However, like any business, dropshipping is not without its challenges and pitfalls.

By learning from the mistakes of others, you can avoid common pitfalls and set your business up for success. Some common mistakes include choosing the wrong niche, failing to conduct proper market research, not setting up your website properly, not managing your inventory effectively, and not providing top-notch customer service.

To avoid these mistakes, it's important to do your research, plan ahead, and stay organized. Make sure you choose a profitable niche and conduct thorough market research to understand your target audience. Take the time to set up your website properly, and make sure you have reliable suppliers and a system in place for managing your inventory.

Additionally, providing excellent customer service is key to keeping your customers happy and returning for future purchases. Be transparent about shipping and return policies, and make sure you have a system in place for handling returns and refunds.

Finally, don't forget to keep track of your finances and stay on top of legal and tax issues to avoid any legal troubles down the line.

Its Do-able , You can Do it!!

Dropshipping can be a lucrative and rewarding business venture with low startup costs and the potential for significant profits. By choosing the right niche, identifying your target audience, building a professional website, finding reliable suppliers, and effectively marketing your products, you can start and grow a successful dropshipping business. It's important to stay on top of inventory management, customer service, and financial tracking to ensure long-term success. With dedication, hard work, and a willingness to learn from mistakes, anyone can become a successful dropshipper. So go ahead and take the first step towards your entrepreneurial journey and start your dropshipping business today!

xxxENDxxx

If you want a dropshipping website done for you

-Free Hosting for 1 Year

-Free Domain name for 1 year

-Fully intergrated with Aliexpress, Alibaba, Amazon, Ebay etc

-Fully intergrated with payment platforms like paypal, Visa, Mastercard, etc

Whatsapp your website budget cost to +254 710 100 974 and we will gladly d one for yu at your budget.

Thank you!